A NOTE TO PARENTS

Reading Aloud with Your Child

Research shows that reading books aloud is the single most valuable support parents can provide in helping children learn to read.

- Be a ham! The more enthusiasm you display, the more your child will enjoy the book.
- Run your finger underneath the words as you read to signal that the print carries the story.
- Leave time for examining the illustrations more closely; encourage your child to find things in the pictures.
- Invite your youngster to join in whenever there's a repeated phrase in the text.
- Link up events in the book with similar events in your child's life.
- If your child asks a question, stop and answer it. The book can be a means to learning more about your child's thoughts.

Listening to Your Child Read Aloud

The support of your attention and praise is absolutely crucial to your child's continuing efforts to learn to read.

- If your child is learning to read and asks for a word, give it immediately so that the meaning of the story is not interrupted. DO NOT ask your child to sound out the word.
- On the other hand, if your child initiates the act of sounding out, don't intervene.
- If your child is reading along and makes what is called a miscue, listen for the sense of the miscue. If the word "road" is substituted for the word "street," for instance, no meaning is lost. Don't stop the reading for a correction.
- If the miscue makes no sense (for example, "horse" for "house"), ask your child to reread the sentence because you're not sure you understand what's just been read.
- Above all else, enjoy your child's growing command of print and make sure you give lots of praise. *You are your child's first teacher—and the most important one. Praise from you is critical for further risk-taking and learning.*

—Priscilla Lynch
Ph.D., New York University
Educational Consultant

To E.W.R.
—W.R.

To my mom and dad, who from the very beginning supported me in my desire to draw, and to the memory of my grandfather, who showed me the magic of nature.
—J.C.

Text copyright © 1994 by Walter Retan.
Illustrations copyright © 1994 by Jean Cassels.
All rights reserved. Published by Scholastic Inc.
HELLO READER! and CARTWHEEL BOOKS are registered trademarks of Scholastic Inc.

Library of Congress Cataloging-in-Publication Data

Retan, Walter,
Armies of ants / by Walter Retan : illustrated by Jean Cassels.
p.   cm. — (Hello reader! Level 4)
ISBN 0-590-47616-5
1. Ants—Juvenile literature. [1. Ants.] I. Cassels, Jean. ill. II. Title. III. Series.
QL568.F7R46   1994   93-29782
595.79'6—dc20   CIP   AC

40 39 38 37 36 35 34   6 7 8 9/0

Printed in the U.S.A.   23

First Scholastic printing, May 1994

Armies
of Ants

by Walter Retan
Illustrated by Jean Cassels

Hello Reader!—Level 4

SCHOLASTIC INC.
New York Toronto London Auckland Sydney

CHAPTER 1
Ants on the March

The morning sun shines
above the hot rain forest.
Something strange is going on
under the tall, green trees.
A soft hissing sound rises
from the forest floor.
Insects leap into the air.
They hit against tree trunks.
Flies buzz close to the ground.
And every now and then,
a bird swoops down
to grab an insect.
What is happening here?
An army of ants is
on the march!

These are army ants.
They live in the hot,
wet parts of Africa and
South America.
These ants feed on almost any
kind of insect or small animal
in their path — from grasshoppers
and spiders to nesting birds.

One army ant alone cannot do
much harm.
But hundreds of thousands
of them are a dangerous enemy.
Working together, they sting
their prey.
They use their strong jaws
and sharp teeth to cut
into it.
Then they share the food.

Army ants do not build nests.
They stay in a different place
every night — under a rock,
in a log, or in a tree trunk.
They form a kind of living net.
They use their strong claws to
hook their legs and bodies
together.
They rest in a huge ball.
In the morning, they separate
and start off on the hunt again.
They might march in a straight line
or in a fan shape.
There are no real leaders.
One group of ants will lead
the way for a short distance.
Then another group crowds
to the front and takes over.
This push of ants from behind
keeps the swarm moving forward.

The largest soldier ants
stay on the outside.
These ants protect
the rest of the swarm
from enemies.
Every few weeks, the ants
stop moving.
It's time for the queen ant
to lay her eggs.

The queen is the biggest ant
in the colony.
The ants choose a safe place and
gather around their queen.
Some of the worker ants find food
to share with the other ants.
Soon the queen lays many
thousands of eggs.
After about three weeks, the army
goes on the march again.

CHAPTER 2
Ants Have Outlived the Dinosaurs

Army ants are not the only
amazing members of the
ant family.
There are about 9,000 kinds
of ants living all over
the world.
The only places without ants
are cold and icy — like the
Arctic and Antarctic.

Ants have been around since
before the days of the dinosaurs.
Dinosaurs died out millions
of years ago.
But ants are still here!

There are thousands of kinds
of ants.
But their bodies all follow
the same basic design.
An ant's head is usually large.
Two long feelers, or antennas,
stretch out from the front
of the head.
An ant uses its feelers to smell,
recognize other ants,
and examine pieces of food.

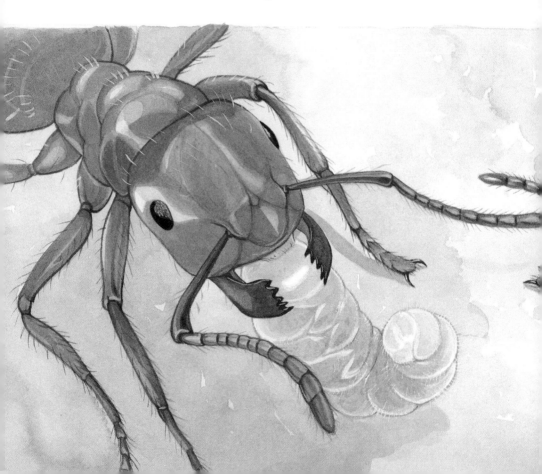

When an ant is busy, its feelers
are always moving.
The head also includes the jaws.
Instead of moving up and down
as our jaws do, an ant's jaws
open to the side.
Ants use their jaws to pick up
food, carry their young, and
fight enemies.
Many ants have sharp teeth
in their jaws.

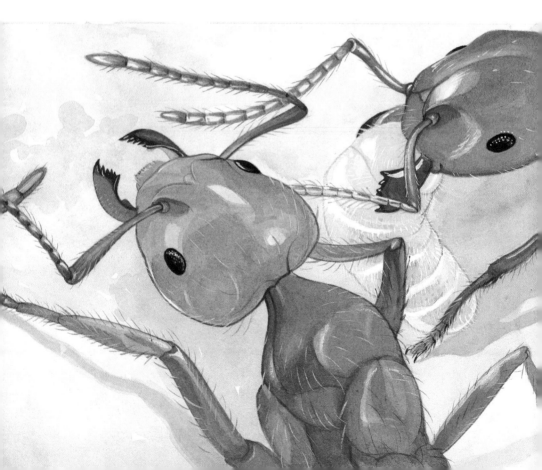

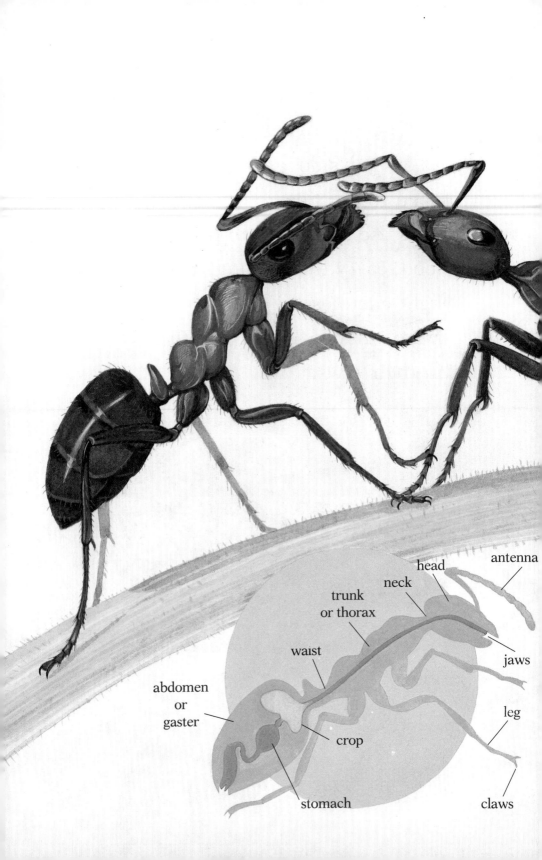

antenna

head

neck

trunk
or thorax

waist

jaws

abdomen
or
gaster

crop

leg

stomach

claws

A thin neck connects
the ant's head to its trunk.
Three pairs of legs are attached
to the trunk.
The foot of each leg
has two hooked claws.
Ants use their claws to climb trees,
dig up dirt, and fight enemies.

The ant's thin waist connects the
trunk to its abdomen or gaster.
The gaster holds the ant's stomach
and a special pouch for storing food.
This pouch is called the crop.
An ant can spit up food that is
in the crop and share it
with other ants.
The crop stretches easily
to make space
for more food.

CHAPTER 3
Strong Poison

Some kinds of ants have a poisonous
stinger at the end of the gaster.
The bulldog ant of Australia is one
of the most dangerous ants.
This ant hunts alone.
It hides under a low bush and
waits for insects.
When one comes along, the
bulldog ant leaps out and grabs
the insect in its strong jaws.
The ant pushes its poisonous stinger
deep into the insect.
Then it tears its dead prey
into pieces.
Bulldog ants can run very fast.
They will even chase people!

The fire ant is also a stinging ant.
It has made its way into the
United States from South America.
The fire ant's stinger feels like a
red-hot needle jabbing the skin.
Fire ants are a big problem
for farmers.
They build large nest mounds
in fields so farmers have
a hard time cutting their hay.
Fire ants also sting cows.

Some poisonous ants don't have
a stinger.
They have a poison gland
inside the gaster.
They squirt the poison at their
enemies from an opening at the
tip of the gaster.

CHAPTER 4
Working Together

Ants are social insects.
They live together in groups
called colonies.
Different ants in the colony
have different jobs.
They work together for the good
of the whole group.
The most important member of
any ant colony is the queen.
When queen ants are born,
they have four wings.
So do the male ants.
As soon as they are old enough,
the queens and the males fly high
into the air and mate.
Soon afterward the males die.

Each queen flies off to start
her own colony.
First she sheds her wings.
Then she finds a good place
to build a nest.
She lays her eggs in this nest.
Ant eggs are so tiny that
people usually cannot see them.
In a few days the queen's eggs
hatch into *larvae* (LAR-vee).
They have no legs.

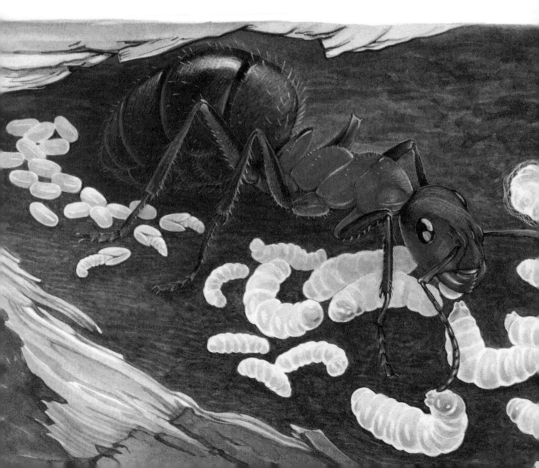

Soon some of the larvae spin
white, silky cocoons; others
grow a thick, clear case.
This is called the *pupal*
(PEW-pull) stage.
After a few weeks, the adult ants
come out of their cocoons or cases.
Female worker ants are usually the
first ones born.
They will gather food, defend
the colony, and repair the nest.

CHAPTER 5
Ant Cities

Ants build many kinds of nests.
Some kinds of black garden ants
make their homes underground.
They use the tiny claws on their
feet to dig tunnels and rooms
in the dirt.
The rooms have different purposes.
Some are for storing food.
Other rooms hold the eggs
and the larvae.
If a room gets too hot or
too cold or too wet, worker ants
will move the eggs and the
larvae to another room.
There is usually a special room for the
queen ant and her newest eggs.
Thousands and thousands of ants
often live together in one
underground home.

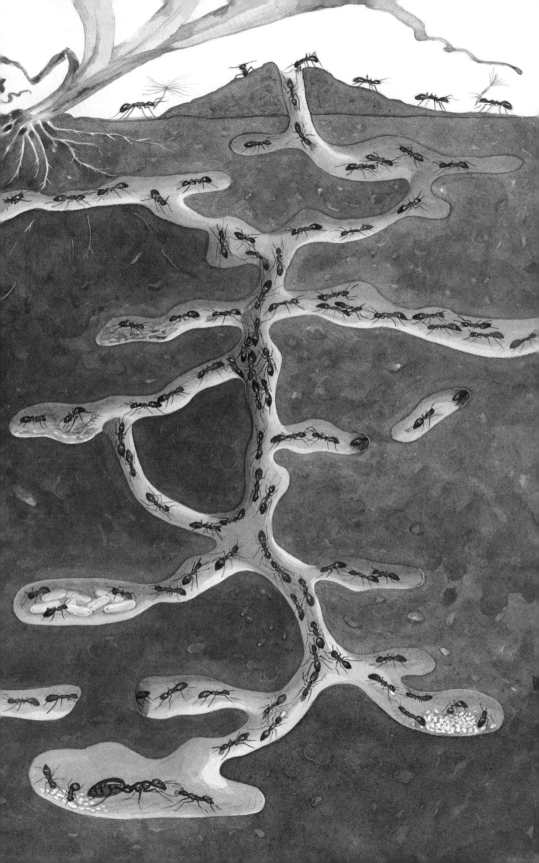

Many kinds of red ants
live in the woods.
Some start their nests
underground.
Then they add a large anthill
above ground.
They pile up dead leaves,
dirt, and pine needles and
weave them together.
The nest has many tunnels and
rooms.
In warm weather, the ants live
above ground.
During the winter, they move
underground.

Carpenter ants make their nests
in the trunks and branches of trees.
Sometimes carpenter ants build nests
in the wooden beams of houses.
When they chew tunnels in healthy
trees or house beams, they
can cause much damage.

The cleverest nest builders are
the weaver ants.
They live in treetops in Africa,
Asia, and Australia.
One colony of weaver ants often
lives in four or five trees.
There may be half a million
members in the colony.
Weaver ants make their nests
by pulling several leaves
together to form a pocket.

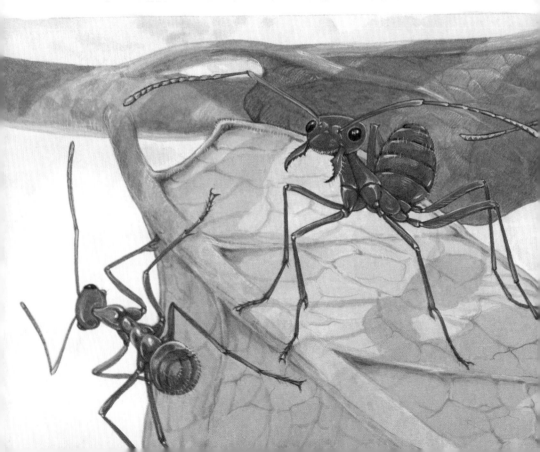

One group lines up
on the edge of a leaf.
These ants hold onto the leaf
with their rear feet.
Then they grab a nearby
leaf in their jaws.
If the distance is too great,
the workers form chains.
Each ant holds onto the waist
of the ant in front of it.

While this group of ants holds
the leaf edges together,
another group brings out the
larvae.
Each worker ant gently holds a
larva (LAR-vuh) in its jaws.
The larva lets out a small
bit of silk that sticks
to the leaf's edge.
The worker carries the
larva to the edge
of the second leaf.
This draws out the silk
from the larva
like a thread and binds
the two leaves together.
The nest, hanging from
the branches, looks like
a silken leafy cocoon.

Some kinds of ants can't build
their own nests or take care
of their young.
They keep slaves to do their work.
Amazon ants are an example
of this kind of ant.
They are very large, with bright-
red or black, shiny bodies.
Their jaws are big and curved.
They can't use them to dig in the earth
or pick up their larvae or pupas.

They can't even get their
own food.
Their slave workers have
to feed them and take care
of the nest.
At home, the Amazon ants are
very lazy.
They hang around the nest
cleaning their shiny bodies
or begging their slaves for food.

But when Amazon ants
look for slaves, they turn
into brave fighters.
As soon as an Amazon ant
finds a nest that belongs to
another kind of ant,
it quickly returns home.
Its body leaves a
special smell on the ground
along the way.

The other Amazon ants
follow this smelly trail
straight to the other nest.
They attack the other ants
and carry away their cocoons.
The young are then raised
by the slave workers
back at the home nest.

CHAPTER 6
Food for Ants

Ants eat many different kinds
of foods.
Army ants eat insects
and other small animals.
Harvester ants gather the seeds
from plants such as wheat.
They carry the seeds to their nest
and store them in special rooms.
Worker ants use their jaws
to tear off the hard
seed coverings.
Then they chew the kernels
into a soft pulp.
This is sometimes called ant bread.
Harvester ants always have a supply
of seeds and ant bread
in their storerooms.

Leafcutter ants grow their own
food in huge underground nests.
More than a million ants often
live in one nest.
At night, columns of workers leave
the nest.
They cut pieces of leaves
from trees and other plants.
They carry the leaf pieces back to
their nest by holding them above
their heads like umbrellas.

For this reason, they are often called umbrella — or parasol — ants. At the nest, smaller worker ants chop the leaves into tiny pieces. Then other, even smaller, workers chew the bits into a soft mush. They use this mush for growing fungus in underground gardens. The ants then feed on the fungus.

Silver ants in the Sahara desert
in Africa hunt at high noon.
They avoid their enemies, who are
hiding from the noontime heat.
A silver ant hunts alone.
It looks for insects and
tiny animals that have died
from the heat.
Silver ants' legs are much
longer than the legs
of most other ants.

Their long legs raise them up
and away from the hot sand.
These ants move very fast.
They try not to touch
the ground too often or
for too long.
Sometimes they hold two
of their legs in the air
as they hip-hop along.

Honey ants live in the southwestern
part of the United States.
During cool, wet weather,
the worker ants gather
a sweet liquid called honeydew
from flowers and other insects.
They store it in their crops
until they are back at their nest.
There they spit the honeydew
into the mouths of large, young
workers.
These workers are called *repletes*
(ruh-PLETES).
Their crops stretch and stretch
as they fill with honeydew.
The repletes become so big
that they can't move.
During hot, dry weather,
honeydew is hard to find.
But hungry workers just go
to the repletes.
A replete will spit up honeydew
into a hungry worker's mouth.

CHAPTER 7
If All the Ants Disappeared

There are millions of billions
of ants in the world.
Life on earth would be different
if they disappeared. Here's why:

- Ants eat huge numbers of insect pests.

- Ants scatter seeds.

- Ants eat the dead bodies of many insects and small animals.

- Other animals such as frogs,
  toads, woodpeckers, lizards,
  and anteaters eat ants for food.
- Ants stir up the soil, enriching it.
  Without ants to do this job,
  plants and forests would die.
  Animals that eat the plants
  for food would also die.
  Thousands of kinds of plants
  and animals would slowly
  vanish from the earth.

Of course, some ants can be pests.
But, overall, ants do far more good
than bad.

Ants are very special insects.
They can communicate with
each other.
They divide up their work to
carry out hard jobs.
And ants work for the good
of the whole group.

The ant also has been successful
because it is such a tiny insect.
Other, much bigger animals —
like the dinosaurs —
have come and gone.
But the ants are still here!